A Guide to Keith Johnstone's
GORILLA THEATRE™

Published 2017 by the International Theatrsports™ Institute (ITI)

215 - 36 Avenue NE, Unit 6 | Calgary, AB | T2E 2L4 | CANADA

Copyright © 2017 ITI

This guide is in no way a replacement for performance rights.
Non performance rights holders wishing to perform the Gorilla Theatre™ format should apply at:
admin@theatresports.org

Layout: Dagmar Bauer konzipiert & gestaltet, Stuttgart, Germany
Illustrations by fotolia.com

Cover Photograph: Improoperatørene 📷 by Jonathan Stone

»The struggle to attain your vision is at

the heart of Gorilla Theatre™

and makes it unlike any other form.«

CONTENTS

- **8 INTRODUCTION**
- 8 About This Guide
- 8 About Keith Johnstone
- 9 About the ITI
- 9 Before Playing Gorilla Theatre™

- **10 GORILLA THEATRE™ BACKGROUND**
- 10 What is Gorilla Theatre™?
- 11 The Beginning of Gorilla Theatre™
- 13 What Gorilla Theatre™ Can Achieve

- **14 IMPORTANT CONCEPTS**
- 14 The Spirit
- 15 Embracing Failure
- 16 Teamwork
- 17 Mischief and Misbehaviour

- **18 LET'S BEGIN**
- 18 Creative Aims of Gorilla Theatre™
- 19 What You Need for Basic Gorilla
- 19 Starting the Show

- **22 GORILLA THEATRE™ IN MORE DETAIL**
- 22 Directing
- 22 Themes / Vision
- 23 Fighting for Your Scene
- 25 Taking the Stage as Director
- 25 Variety & Shape of Show
- 26 Directing Advice
- 27 Art of Storytelling / Terminology
- 28 Enforce a Positive Attitude
- 28 Remove Defensive Blocking
- 28 Eliminate Bridging
- 28 Force Transitions
- 28 Explore Latent Material
- 28 Combine Elements
- 28 Enforce Recapitulation
- 29 Suggest Corrective Games
- 29 Canceling
- 29 Wimping
- 29 Hedging
- 29 Sidetracking
- 29 Gossip
- 30 How to Move Scenes Forward by Directing / Side Coaching
- 30 Ending Scenes
- 31 Suggestions on How to End Scenes
- 32 Rationing the Directing Time
- 32 The Gorilla
- 33 Playing the Gorilla
- 34 Performing with the Gorilla
- 34 Preparing the Costume
- 35 Not Using a Gorilla
- 36 Drawing Heat
- 38 The Emcee (Master of Ceremonies)
- 38 Voting
- 39 Bananas
- 40 Forfeits
- 40 Creating Forfeits
- 41 Forfeit Tips
- 41 A List of Useful Forfeits
- 42 Winning

- **44 ATTENTION TO DETAIL**
- 44 Tips on Training Gorilla Directors
- 44 Tips on Directing
- 45 Add Theatricality and Spectacle to the Show
- 45 Masks
- 45 Playing Masks
- 45 Directing Masks
- 46 Scenography

- **50 FINAL THOUGHTS**
- 50 Tips From Groups Playing Gorilla
- 51 Memorable Gorilla Moments

- **54 RESOURCES**
- 54 Keith Johnstone's Books
- 54 Keith Johnstone's Newsletters
- 54 DVDs
- 54 Workshops & Training
- 55 Gorilla Mask

INTRO-DUCTION

ABOUT THIS GUIDE

We hope you find this guidebook to be a useful resource for information and inspiration for Gorilla Theatre™. This guide has been created to provide assistance for groups just starting out, clarity for those unsure if they are heading in the right direction, and also a reminder for groups who have been playing a long time to check in on their progress and development.

Here you will find information about the history of Gorilla Theatre™, the skills needed to play, the spirit and theory behind the concept, as well as practical information on the structure and tips on how to play the format.

Most of the material in this study guide comes directly from Keith Johnstone via his book Impro For Storytellers and his 'Gorilla and Micetro' November 1998 newsletter. The commentary and additional material is provided by improvisers from all over the world, some of whom have worked with Keith over the past 40 years, and groups that perform Gorilla Theatre™.

This guide focuses on Gorilla Theatre™, however, we encourage you to build your improvisation skills in general through study with informed teachers. A list of suggested teachers can be found at https://theatresports.org/teachers/ Various resources are also located in a section at the end of this guide.

Enjoy your journey into the world of Gorilla Theatre™ and may you find the fun, inspiration, and great potential this format has to offer.

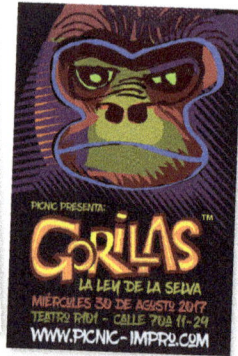

 ITI – **I**nspire **T**he **I**mproviser!

ABOUT KEITH JOHNSTONE

Keith Johnstone was born in 1933 in Devon, England. He grew up hating school, finding that it blunted his imagination. The Royal Court Theatre commissioned a play from him, and he continued to work there from 1956 to 1966, as a play-reader, director and drama teacher, ending as an Associate Director. In his classes he began to question the impact schooling had on his imagination by exploring the reversal of all that his teachers had told him in an attempt to create more spontaneous theatre actors. It was at this time that Keith developed a series of improvisational exercises to help playwrights overcome writers block and for actors to work more spontaneously.

He founded the improvisation group The Theatre Machine in the 1960s, which toured Europe and North America and was invited by the Canadian Government to perform at Expo 67. Keith moved to Calgary, Alberta, Canada in the 1970s and in 1977 co-founded the Loose Moose Theatre Company.

Keith invented the Impro System and improvisation shows such as Gorilla Theatre™, Maestro Impro™, Life Game and Theatresports™. Theatresports™ has become a staple of modern improvisational comedy and is the inspiration for television shows such as 'Whose Line Is It Anyway?'.

top left:
Impro Melbourne
Design Mike Bryant
Melbourne, Australia

top middle:
ZoèTeatri
Modena, Italy

top right:
Picnic Impro
Bogota, Colombia

He is a Professor Emeritus of the University of Calgary. His books, IMPRO and IMPRO FOR STORYTELLERS, outsold Stanislavsky in Germany. He is a playwright of children's productions and both short and full-length adult plays which have been performed in Europe, North America, Africa and South America. Stanford University is home to The Keith Johnstone Papers which consist of original plays, writings, correspondence, theatrical materials, journals, artwork etc. To be more specific, it includes early chapter drafts of IMPRO and IMPRO FOR STORYTELLERS (incl. early writings & drafts on Theatresports™), and some of Keith's original letters (including letters to Keith from Del Close, Peter Coyote, Samuel Beckett, Harold Pinter, Anthony Stirling, Royal Court colleagues, Theatre Machine members etc.). It also includes many of Keith's earliest short stories, documents from his years with the Royal Court, the Theatre Machine and the Loose Moose Theatre, plus newspaper clippings, reviews, programs, photos, letters, artwork and posters.

Keith Johnstone by Frank Totino

ABOUT THE ITI

In 1998, the International Theatresports™ Institute (I.T.I.) was created. It is the organization to which Keith Johnstone has entrusted the legacy of the format Theatresports™. The ITI is a Membership Association of groups and individuals joined together by a shared passion for the work of Keith Johnstone. Those groups who perform any of the formats: Theatresports™, Maestro Impro™ and Gorilla Theatre™, do so after applying for and being approved for performance rights. Rights are extremely inexpensive. Schools are required to have them for copyright reasons but there are no fees attached. The ITI manages the licensing of the formats to these groups and provides resources for learning and development in the field of improvisation. Fees collected from performance rights go towards managing the ITI, giving support and passing on benefits to its members. Keith Johnstone has always refused to take any money from Theatresports™ royalties. The ITI is here to support you and answer any questions you may have regarding Keith's work, including improvisation techniques, games and the Gorilla Theatre™ format itself.

BEFORE PLAYING GORILLA THEATRE™

Gorilla Theatre™ is a copyright format, so before you begin, please contact the ITI and request the rights. The process is easy and in receiving the rights you become a member of the ITI community. This provides you with the format guide, Keith Johnstone newsletters, discounts to our conferences and teachers, and connection to an international network of improvisers who are working with the same ideas and philosophy you are.
Please contact us at admin@theatresports.org or visit theatresports.org

GORILLA THEATRE™ BACKGROUND

WHAT IS GORILLA THEATRE™?

» **The struggle** of the directors to attain their vision of the scene that they imagine (which can equally be rewarding for us when they fail) is at the heart of Gorilla Theatre™ and makes it unlike any other form. Your 'Jane Austen' nineteenth-century scene where players pine for each other but daren't even touch is likely to be hysterically funny, rather than romantic – but whether you achieve your vision or not, there's a huge difference between a director who sets up an Impro-game and does nothing to ensure it's success, and a director who struggles to achieve an authentic 'Jane Austen' scene, or 'Star Trek' scene or 'Nazi Submarine' scene that's more than an amusing waste of time. «   *Keith Johnstone*

A small cast of 3 to 5 performers act as the directors, actors, emcee and scenographers for the scenes. The audience judges the directors on their directing skills. They win a banana as a reward or a forfeit as a punishment. The directors are competing with each other to win a week of quality time with the gorilla. Gorilla Theatre™ is a format for experienced improvisers. Gorilla requires performing and directing expertise, competence in how to work an audience and how to draw 'heat', an understanding of how to perform with a 'gorilla character' (similar to working with mask) and a knack for creating a show with variety. Improvisers must also know how to play 'mock' competition for the audience's entertainment while still supporting each other's work.

*Impro Melbourne
Melbourne, Australia
by John Desengano*

» *Gorilla Theatre™ has a unique blend of form and freedom. I love having the ability to craft original scenarios and dynamics based around a theme and the fast-paced action that propels you from scene to scene. As you move from host to director to player duties, you also get to truly build rapport with the audience and connect in a more nuanced way.* «   *David Charles, SAK Theatre, Orlando, USA*

» **Gorilla Theatre™** is not intended for beginners, and even a good improviser may be a poor coach (although the game will gradually teach the skills). «   *Keith Johnstone,
Gorilla and Maestro Newsletter '98*

THE BEGINNING OF GORILLA THEATRE™

Gorilla Theatre™ debuted in the summer of 1992 at The Loose Moose Theatre Company.

>> **A Loose Moose All-Star Show** was presented using four experienced improvisers, but whether the players were lovers, homeless people or priests, everything was reduced to light-hearted trivia (as per usual). I suggested that we should announce a theme, and invite the audience to shout 'forfeit' if a scene failed to embody it. Such forfeits would involve serving the bar during the interval (for a couple of minutes), or creating a modern dance, or apologizing sincerely to the audience, or whatever.

This led to the 'Theme and Forfeit' game in which themes were chalked on a large wheel, E.g. Religion, Ecology, Forgiveness etc. (different themes for each game). Each player in turn directed a scene selected by spinning the wheel. The spectators either cheered the director if they felt that the scene had adequately expressed the theme of 'Greed', of 'The Future', or whatever, or shouted 'forfeit' if they thought that it hadn't.

Loose Moose Theatre Company
Calgary, Canada
📷 *by Kate Ware*

It was never enough to allow the players in a scene to just chat about the theme. To please the spectators you had to find some dramatic device that expressed the theme. If the scene was about the future perhaps an antique dealer from the future could be caught when she was putting your everyday objects into a sack. The theme of religion might involve a beetle asking if you were God (the 'small voice' game). The theme of 'death' might involve a skeleton wrestling with an old lady who was refusing to die until the entire family was assembled.
It was a difficult skill, but well worth learning, and it was a relief to be watching scenes that had some point. Then I saw a dismal All-Star Show that was especially embarrassing because we had intended it to be an example of excellent Impro to inspire the students at the Loose Moose Summer School.
The show was so bad that the players at the side were looking at their feet and clutching their heads, or were staring into the audience. The message they were giving was 'what's happening on-stage is nothing to do with us'.

GORILLA THEATRE™ BACKGROUND

Shocked by this failure to help each other, I removed the wheel (as not relevant to the current problem) and added someone in a gorilla suit. The audience shouted 'banana' or 'forfeit' after each scene, and the winner was the player who was awarded the most bananas.

The gorilla could entertain the spectators before the show started, and shake hands with them when they left the theatre. It could be a rug in a domestic scene, or your blind date, or could enter with a broom and sweep a failing scene off of the stage, and whenever the audience shouted 'forfeit' it brought a jar of forfeits onto the stage.

The gorilla didn't dominate the game; it accompanied the game. It 'helped out'. It did what was 'needed'. It was not the 'star' of the show. It was a random element that inspired the actors and pleased the audience. Like Harpo - from the Marx Brothers - it never spoke.

The fact that people were prepared to spend two hours in a sometimes not so clean gorilla suit was a testament to the morale of the company. «

Keith Johnstone

» *Keith would come and watch the All-Star Show on Saturdays, where the performers would set each other up in scenes. At notes Keith would point out that we would set-up a scene and then not take responsibility for it. If a scene went badly no one would fight to make it better, or wave down the lights, or throw it off and put themselves at the mercy of the audience. Keith basically devised Gorilla so we would have to take responsibility for scenes we set-up and directed.* «

Dennis Cahill, Loose Moose Theatre Company, Calgary, Canada

» **I gave notes** and suggested the 'directors' who failed to rescue 'bad' scenes should pay a forfeit and directors of 'good' scenes should get some sort of recognition. Gorilla Theatre™ was born at that exact moment. «

Keith Johnstone
News 5 1993

Directing and side-coaching have always been an important part of the Loose Moose Theatre training. Keith directed frequently in his classes and from the judges chair in Theatresports™. Knowing improvisers can miss the obvious or avoid moving stories forward, he encourages everyone in the show to be watching for opportunities to help their fellow players.

» *I believe the gorilla part came from Keith's predilection for animals (i.e. Loose Moose, Micetro) and the bananas naturally fit with the title. Not to mention the possibility of having someone play the gorilla. Once Keith had a problem to solve and a title, the format was more or less complete.* «

Dennis Cahill, Loose Moose Theatre Company, Calgary, Canada

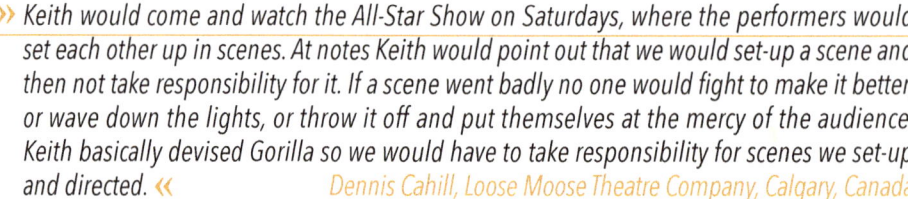

WHAT GORILLA THEATRE™ CAN ACHIEVE

» *It creates a freedom to play, experiment and fail. Some cast members experienced their first moments of performing completely free from anxiety during Gorilla! The onstage mischief and relationships between directors really bond a cast and create exactly the right playful environment you need for good Impro to happen.* «
Cam Percy, Impro Mafia
Brisbane, Australia

Gorilla Theatre™ can
- Develop skills in
   - directing
   - performance
   - storytelling / narrative
   - good natured benevolence and mischief
   - awareness of show shape, variety and content
   - building relationships with the audience
   - full mask work
   - theatricality (props, set, staging, audience interaction)
- Create memorable improvised theatre
- Teach improvisers to care about the work they are creating
- Explore a blend of naturalistic and non-naturalistic theatre with a touch of spectacle

top left:
Contemporary Theater
Rhode Island, USA
by Neal Leaheey

right:
Loose Moose Theatre Company
Calgary, Canada
by Breanna Kennedy

» *I know that my work, both as a teacher, and performer, got better once I started playing Gorilla. Having to look at a scene through different eyes, outside eyes, and ask, "What does this need right now?" is invaluable.* «
Rebecca Northan, Spontaneous Theatre, Toronto, Canada
Loose Moose Theatre alumna

IMPORTANT CONCEPTS

>> *When playing any of Keith's formats, it is important to understand why the show is designed the way it is, and the philosophy that lies behind it. For us it was helpful to get assistance from a good coach who is familiar with Gorilla, and who could help us root out misunderstandings and make the work less safe.* <<
Emil Husby, Improoperatørene, Trondheim, Norway

THE SPIRIT

Keith's work is a specific approach to Impro and performance. The spirit of the work forms the foundation on which the show structure (format) is based.

Aspects of the 'spirit' include:
- Playfulness
- Supporting your partner and valuing their ideas
- Risk taking and bravery
- Honesty and vulnerability
- Being positive
- Failure - Learning to fail gracefully and good-naturedly
- Teamwork
- Misbehaviour
- Storytelling
- Exploring improvisation that is challenging

>> **At first** *the players earned forfeit after forfeit, but this didn't depress anyone because the spectators were gleefully anticipating the moment when they would take their revenge and the players felt absolved.* <<
Keith Johnstone
Impro For Storytellers pg.39

>> *Performed as it was intended there are great layered possibilities of play. The scene work aims at variety so it stretches the performing and directing skills. The interaction between directors, if played with playful misbehaviour, has some great moments of collaborative clown work.* <<

Shawn Kinley
Loose Moose Theatre Company, Calgary, Canada

MITICO Festival and ITI conference - Milano, Italy 📷 by Tiffany Schultz

EMBRACING FAILURE

>> *To explore a new idea means taking a risk and in order to take that risk we need to accept the possibility of failure. Safety and repetition do not equal success, they are easy choices to cope with fear. Letting fear guide your artistic choices is the real failure as you limit possibilities.* <<

Patti Stiles, Impro Melbourne, Melbourne, Australia
Loose Moose Theatre, RFT, Die Nasty alumna

In our society failure is a concept laden with negative connotations. In a world based on 'be the best', this message builds a great deal of stress and puts focus on success. Yet we know scientifically, that through failure we learn.

We equate laughter from the audience with success in improvisation yet the search for this type of praise generates 'light hearted trivial' work. Improvisers are caught in a vicious cycle of repetition, using and reusing any moment, gag, pop culture reference or gimmick they have found, or have seen others do, that 'works'.

In order for an improviser to play freely they must embrace the possibilities of glory or disaster. Embracing failure gives us the opportunity to show the audience a very special creature: the fearless, good-natured improviser who ventures willingly into the unknown, an improviser who, regardless of the outcome of their scene, maintains sparkles of joy in their eyes.

>> **The reason** why so few people understand the value of failure, is that it is usually tied to horrible self-punishment which has nothing to do with learning (muscle tension probably makes learning more difficult) and is purely defensive. <<

Keith Johnstone
Theatresports™ and Lifegame Newsletter - Issue Number 1, 1989

IMPORTANT CONCEPTS

>> *Fail, fail and fail again. After each scene you rehearse, ask the director whether they got what they wanted. Ask the players whether they felt inspired, and when. Once you've built trust with your cast, take outlandish risks in rehearsal. Aim to make two big mistakes per performance.* << *Cam Percy, Impro Mafia, Brisbane, Australia*

>> **The only way** *to learn is to fail. Failing and staying happy is the quickest way to demonstrate good nature and make the audience love you.* << *Keith Johnstone*

Loose Moose Theatre Company - Calgary, Canada
by Kate Ware

TEAMWORK

Picnic Impro - Bogota, Colombia
by Fernanda Pineda

>> *Performers in Gorilla swap hats throughout the performance, serving as hosts (emcee), directors/playwrights, and players. This intensity is both challenging and incredibly rewarding as you must develop and sharpen numerous elements of your skill set. There is very little, if any, true offstage time in a Gorilla performance and this quickly builds an intense ensemble.* << *David Charles, SAK Theatre, Orlando, USA*

Improvisation technique is built on teamwork. We accept and support each other's ideas so we can explore these ideas freely. It isn't about your individual glory, but a focus on working with each other to give the audience a good show. When everyone works for the show instead of for themselves the audience is rewarded with a benevolent experience. Gorilla Theatre™ is an ensemble show requiring teamwork from ALL of the performers, technicians, volunteers and audience. Everyone must be focused on everything: how to look after each other, how to make each scene work and the overall needs of the show.

>> *Trust. Trust and play with each other. Know how to interact with each other. Sometimes the show will wait if you are honestly WITH your partner in true interaction.* << *Shawn Kinley, Loose Moose Theatre Company Calgary, Canada*

MISCHIEF AND MISBEHAVIOUR

>> *The director has done an elegant job at the beginning and there's an easy field to play on. I've had quite a few however (especially with Dennis Cahill) that were marked with such massive misbehaviour that it was difficult for the audience to get themselves back under control. In that case it's the "clown" work that I appreciate. You find who you are in relation to others in the work naturally like good Commedia Dell Arte where certain characters will almost always have the same relationship in each show regardless of the improvisation, and the audience is engaged in that.* <<
Shawn Kinley, Loose Moose Theatre Company
Calgary, Canada

Connected to the spirit of the work, Keith always encourages a balanced amount of misbehaviour in his formats. He wants the audience to see the players as "happy, benevolent creatures, released from their cages once a week, sometimes a little difficult to control". Play and misbehaviour add to the experience as long as it is in good spirit.

One could play mischief by playfully fighting the director if the director is unclear in their set up, or if the director isn't helping the scene. When it gets to the point of the players rising up against the director and performing mutiny, it can be a thrilling event but that should only happen a maximum of one or two times per show. The principle relationship between director and player should be one of awareness, respect and mutual inspiration.

Mean spirited acts like put downs or serious arguments are not in the interest of anyone. Not all the players should misbehave or draw 'heat' in a show, or it loses its impact.

Mischief and misbehaviour are the foundations for understanding the technique of Drawing Heat, which is an important component of Gorilla Theatre™. We look at Drawing Heat in more detail on page 36. Misbehaviour should never disrupt the game. The audience take the game seriously and so should the performers.

i Bugardini - Rome, Italy by Elisa Pizza

>> *Listen to the other directors' themes, vision and direction. Inspire them by helping their vision come to life. The mischief is there to help you when it isn't working, it is not an excuse to avoid telling stories.* <<
Patti Stiles, Impro Melbourne, Melbourne, Australia
Loose Moose Theatre, RFT, Die Nasty alumna

LET'S BEGIN

>> *Pay attention to the details of the format, try to understand why they are there to make the best of them.* <<
Felipe Ortiz, Picnic Impro, Bogota, Clombia

CREATIVE AIMS OF GORILLA THEATRE™

>> *What's special is the element of interaction between directors and actors. I don't know any other format where the drama is highlighted in the struggle to get actors to embody what you envision, or for you to adapt so palpably what you imagined in favour of what was being revealed in the moment.* <<
Steve Jarand, Loose Moose Theatre Company
Calgary, Canada

Loose Moose Theatre Company - Calgary, Canada by Breanna Kennedy

Gorilla Theatre™ teaches improvisers to break through the mediocrity that can happen in improvisation. The format is a platform that provides improvisers a safe place to take risks with the type of scenes (content, themes, ideas) and how to perform those scenes (audience interaction, masks, puppets, double figures, projected images) and the opportunity to tell stories that reflect the world we live in. Gorilla Theatre™ can be a wild ride of hysterically funny scenes and comedic mayhem but this is not its main objective.

>> **... Perhaps** demanding a scene in which a beggar is kicked and turns out to be Jesus, or a passionate love story in which someone makes the wrong choice. <<
Keith Johnstone
Gorilla and Maestro Newsletter '98

>> *In improvisation, we are constantly straddling that line between wanting to serve our characters and deliver strong and committed performances, but also wanting to build the relationship with the audience about who we are as creative individuals. Del Close talked about "Wearing your character lightly, like a hat," for this reason, but in a "fourth wall" format like Harold, this can lead to glib, uncommitted acting styles. Gorilla Theatre™ not only allows players to explicitly say "This is my vision for the next few minutes," but allows a debate about the merits of that to happen, live on the stage, in a way which is frequently incredibly funny.* <<
Tom Salinsky, Spntaneity Shop, London, UK

WHAT YOU NEED FOR BASIC GORILLA

Essential Items
· 3-5 improvisers (too many players changes the nature of the format)
· Forfeits (see forfeit section page 40)
· A forfeit chalice. (A chalice is a goblet or footed cup intended to hold a drink. If you can't find a chalice then you need an object to put your forfeits in which make them look important when presented.)
· A system for scoring using either bananas that you can pin to the player's clothing or a scoreboard that has player names and a place to pin awarded bananas
· A stage, lights, sound

Strongly Recommended Items
· A gorilla suit and 1 improviser to play the gorilla (see Gorilla section on page 34)
· An offstage or backstage area, with a chair, for the gorilla to relax and take the mask off without being seen by the audience.
· A microphone
· Set pieces such as chairs, table, a bed (see Scenography section on page 46)
· A large board that says "the Director responsible for this scene is ____ "

top:
Impro Melbourne - Melbourne, Australia
by John Desengano

left:
Unexpected Productions - Seattle, USA
by Jennifer Matthews

STARTING THE SHOW

>> *Play it a bunch of times until you start to see the patterns, trust each other, and watch the shape of the show as a whole.* <<   *Dave Ware, Loose Moose Theatre Company, Calgary, Canada*

A Gorilla Theatre™ show can be as short as 50 minutes or as long as 2 hours (with intermission). It can be played with or without an emcee. A decision to share the emceeing should be based on the ability of the improvisers to manage the structure of the show, i.e. the voting, while also directing and performing. (See Voting section page 38)

>> **Several experienced players** enter and (if there is no Commentator) one of them becomes a temporary emcee who welcomes the audience, explains the game, and announces that the winner of the game will be awarded a weeks 'quality time' with the 'Gorilla' (as though it is a great privilege). Last week's winner is then introduced, and enters hand in hand with someone wearing a gorilla suit, or perhaps one will be carrying the other. The 'Gorilla' is delighted to see the audience and goes 'ape', perhaps shaking hands with the front row and showing great affection (or mixed feelings) for the player with whom it spent the previous week. <<

Keith Johnstone
Impro For Storytellers pg. 42-43

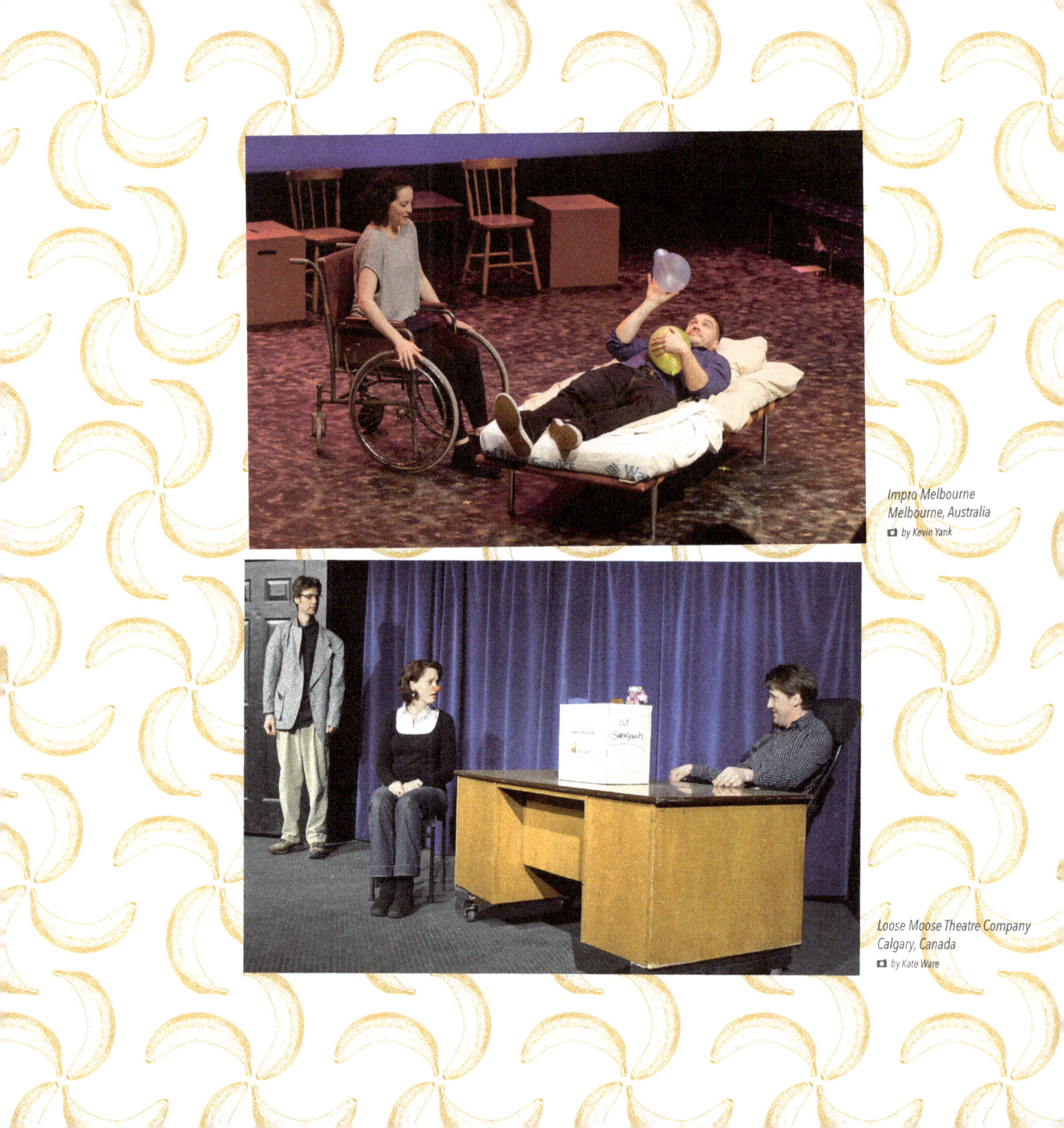

Impro Melbourne
Melbourne, Australia
by Kevin Yank

Loose Moose Theatre Company
Calgary, Canada
by Kate Ware

Improoperatørene - Trondheim, Norway 📷 by Jonathan Stone

GORILLA THEATRE™ IN MORE DETAIL

DIRECTING

>> Take risks, think about the things that you always wanted to try, things of crazy ideas you've had, and try them. <<

Felipe Ortiz, Picnic Impro, Bogota, Colombia

*Again! Productions
Paris, France
by Again! Productions*

The directors provide the initial inspiration to the players with scene starts or ideas.
To stimulate these ideas, preparation for a show could include:
· Looking at who you are playing with and thinking of challenges for the individual improvisers
· Reading the newspaper
· Taking time to think of a subject that interests you and learn a little about it
· Asking yourself "What have I never seen in an improvisation show?" even something as simple as a location could be a wonderful inspiration
· Looking around your house or second hand stores for inspiring objects or costume pieces

Gorilla Theatre™ benefits when the directors put a little thought into the show before hand.

Themes / Vision

>> Have a vision for the evening. I always like to commit to directing scenes with emotional truth, or scenes that highlight a spiritual truth. Something BIG, and worthwhile....that is in contrast to the visions and goals of the other directors. Scenes with a historical viewpoint etc. Always check-in at intermission and ask, "What does the show need now?", "Are there any scenes worth bringing back?<<

*Rebecca Northan, Spontaneous Theatre, Toronto, Canada
Loose Moose Theatre alumna*

It is rare in improvisation to see scenes attacking content that explores life and the human condition. Gorilla Theatre™ offers you, the improviser, opportunities to explore these stories.
As the director you can look at topics or themes that are important to you. The challenge is how to put these ideas on stage. Try something daring or thought provoking. If you fail, accept the forfeit with glee! Why not? You've just had the opportunity to creatively explore an idea and you've learned something.

Impro Melbourne - Melbourne, Australia
by Impro Melbourne

Loose Moose Theatre Company - Calgary, Canada *by Kate Ware*

» **Themes might include**
- Ecology
- Education
- Good families / bad families
- Taboos
- Justice
- Religion
- Romance and lust
- Crime and punishment

If ecology was the theme and the players just gossiped, the audience would give them a forfeit, so the way to survive was to incorporate the theme into the structure: a beetle with a white flag might try to surrender, or a choir of angels could be killed by herbicides. «

Keith Johnstone,
Impro For Storytellers pg. 42-43

» **Boldly announce** what you want at the start of your scene (so that we'll know exactly what you are struggling to achieve), for example:
"I want to see an out of work parent who is too poor to buy a Christmas present for a child." Or
"I want a scene with pathos in which someone is 'stood-up by their date' and comforted by a fatherly waiter!" «

Keith Johnstone,
Gorilla and Maestro Newsletter '98

Fighting for Your Scene

» *Even as a director, you and the performer are partners in the performance. Lose your idea in favour of your partner's inspiration. Fight for your idea in favour of your partner's failings and missteps. Be efficient and benevolent in your directions.* « *Shawn Kinley,*
Loose Moose Theatre Company, Calgary, Canada

» **Fight for your scene** by throwing in dialogue, by starting it again, by recasting it, by ejecting someone and taking over their role (the ultimate insult in professional theatre) and so on. « *Keith Johnstone,*
Gorilla and Maestro Newsletter '98

GORILLA THEATRE™
IN MORE DETAIL

Fighting for your scene does not mean fighting for the idea you've already imagined or forcing improvisers to do things they are uncomfortable with. As a director you must be watching your fellow players to see what inspires and what doesn't, or where they need permission to step into the unknown. As director, be in the moment with the players and the scene.

When you come to the show with ideas, remember these ideas are starting points. The aim is to inspire the improvisers to create a scene on the theme, topic, subject you are aiming towards. The improvisers cannot do the scene you've already imagined, however they can attack the scene or theme you give them. Your job is to direct them to keep them on track, help them when they are unsure, give permission when they look like they want to avoid moving the story forward and help the scene develop when needed.

>> If I say, 'I want a scene dealing with losing a parent', and the improvisers start with two rabbits in a carrot patch, it is my job to get the scene I want. I could ask one player to say, 'Mommy didn't come home last night', or 'Have you ever heard of a thing called a trap?', or 'Did you see the foot the farmer has on his keychain?'. These directions take their starting offer of rabbits and achieve my vision of losing a parent.

If someone starts as a chair in a school classroom, which moves it away from emotion which underlies my vision, I would guess the improviser is either not inspired or being mischievous. I could give them a new clear starting direction. 'It's early Christmas morning, you're 14 years old looking at the tree' or I could stop and recast. Of course I could also use what they are doing and direct them. Say 'I remember being an acorn' or have a student come into class crying and the chair learns about loss via this child's story.

It might sound difficult but it is actually fun to fight for your vision using what is there as inspiration. You don't know what the improvisers might do. It is way more exciting than trying to control the improvisers to do the whole scene you have already imagined. «   *Patti Stiles*
Impro Melbourne, Melbourne, Australia
Loose Moose Theatre, RFT, Die Nasty alumna

Most improvisers will naturally try to avoid moving the story into dangerous territory, yet this is exactly what the audience wants. Dangerous means something might be revealed, and we may get a glimpse into someone's life be it the character, actor or director. This could be falling in love, or holding your baby for the first time, or facing a psychotic killer.

Aim for meaningful rather than trivial content: 'What would your last words be if you were facing the guillotine?' vs. 'the history of cheese.'

i Bugardini - Rome, Italy by Elisa Pizza

Taking the Stage as Director

>> *Directing is a great way of making your partners look good, talk to them, try to see what could be inspiring, surprising, and challenging, it's a collaborative process.* <<
Daniel Orrantia, Picnic Impro, Bogota, Colombia

>> **Players wishing** to direct a scene put their name-card into the 'slot' (which may cause some confusion if several players are competing to direct). Don't let one name push another out of the slot so it falls to the floor – this looks 'messy'. <<
Keith Johnstone,
Gorilla and Maestro Newsletter '98

by Impro Melbourne

Directors do not need to direct in a specific order and you do not need to make it fair, each having the same amount of scenes. Forcing directors to direct in turn is creating a system of control that isn't useful in the show. Besides if one director is having a bad night they can direct less and a director who is 'on' may direct more. Directors should want to direct and running to the board to put their name up shows their enthusiasm and desire to do so.

>> **When directors** have no idea what they want – apart from entertaining the audience – Gorilla Theatre™ is just another way of packaging the 'same old stuff.' But a series of fights to achieve something worthwhile can be wonderful to watch. <<
Keith Johnstone,
Gorilla and Maestro Newsletter '98

Variety & Shape of Show

>> *It was amazing to me to see the variety of scenes audiences will respond to, if only you give them the opportunity.* <<
Cam Percy, Impro Mafia, Brisbane, Australia

*Loose Moose Theatre Company
Calgary, Canada
by Kate Ware*

GORILLA THEATRE™ IN MORE DETAIL

*Smoking Sofa
Paris, France
by Smoking Sofa*

Directors should be looking at the following elements:
- Length: create scenes lasting varying lengths of time
- Type: watch for 'themes' that begin to repeat, 3 love scenes in a row, for example
- Tempo: varying player's rhythms and/or energy
- Stage picture: create different visual pictures
- Number of players: if we've had a few scenes with 2 people, try the whole cast or 1 person
- Music and lighting: these are great gifts, used too often they lose their magic, if not used we loose the possibilities of what they can add
- Emotion: we want the audience to experience a range of emotions

>> *A Gorilla Theatre™ show can encompass everything – short form games, strong scene work, "pimping and dimping", audience interaction, long-form narrative work where successive scenes from the same director advance an ongoing plot, Harold-style edits and reincorporations across the show, physical theatre, straight scenes, genre work. This means *both* that an individual show can contain enormous variety *and* that different Gorilla Theatre™ shows can be very different from each other.* <<   *Tom Salinsky, Spontaneity Shop, London, UK.*

Directing Advice

>> *Surprise each other. Bring props. Do genre stuff. Plant people in the audience. Set up scenes you've never seen done before. Never play the same game twice.* <<   *Tom Salinsky
Spontaneity Shop, London, UK.*

- Good directors resist micro-managing the scene.
- Confident directors will wait and let the players find the scene.
- When a scene is struggling that is the time to give some advice or inspiration. Don't leave the players hanging and uninspired. Even a small stimulation when the players seem lost can keep them reassured.
- When directing the improvisers help, them discover the moment (don't tell them the future).
- Sometimes the simplest directions are the most useful. (see section 'tips on directing / side coaching')
- Choose topics or themes that you have a personal curiosity or point of view about.
- Avoid ideas that are born from 'this will be really funny' or topics based on the possible banana success rate. Winning doesn't prove anything.
- When setting up a scene, remember less is more.
- If you are stuck for ideas, read the newspaper and note what prompts an emotional response in you.

>> *I think it is good to come for the night of the show with a couple of ideas about scenes you would like to direct. It is also good to know that it can happen, depending from how the show is going, that you must give up your ideas and looking for what really the show needs when will be your turn to direct a scene. I suggest also to be suspicious about ideas for scenes that seems to be very clever and cool. In my experience they often lead to an unsatisfactory scene. Maybe because you are more in touch with your idea than with other players.* <<

Giuseppe Marchei, i Bugardini, Rome, Italy

ART OF STORYTELLING - TERMINOLOGY

>> *You must know how to direct. You're not sitting on the outside asking yourself, "If I were in the scene, what would I say right now?" I've seen beginner Gorilla players try to "improvise from the outside" like that, rather than telescoping out to look for opportunities for dramatic action, narrative, or unfulfilled promises to the audience.* <<

*Rebecca Northan
Spontaneous Theatre, Toronto, Canada
Loose Moose Theatre alumna*

>> **Directors need** to understand the art of story-telling, and they must be able to identify the defences improvisers are using and intervene to remove them. <<

*Keith Johnstone,
News 5 1993*

SAK Theatre - Orlando, USA by Emmi Green

Over the years Keith has created terminology to pinpoint the damage we do to stories as we improvise. As Gorilla Theatre™ is designed for more experienced improvisers, the assumption is that players already have an understanding of basic terms. We'll now take a look at some terms specifically from a director's point of view with suggestions on how to move a story forward.

GORILLA THEATRE™ IN MORE DETAIL

The following comes from Keith Johnstone's newsletter: News 5 1993

>> **Enforce a Positive Attitude:** Many players protect themselves by being negative. (This positive / negative terminology isn't very satisfactory but it is the best I've come up with). If someone says 'What a boring film that was.' interrupt them and get them to say: 'What a wonderful film that was!'.

Remove Defensive Blocking: 'Is the door to the lion's cage supposed to be open like that?' 'Oh yes, it's always open.' Directors should interrupt and force a response like: 'Oh no! The lion's on the loose!' Then the action may move forward.

Eliminate Bridging: You bridge when you avoid taking the obvious next step. Nervous improvisers always like to have something in reserve. Beware of this and if a parcel arrives, and there is a delay in opening it, please shout: 'Open the parcel'. If the players are moving towards some sort of love scene and the phone rings, or an old boyfriend arrives, interrupt and take the action back a little way and say: 'Get on with the love scene!'

Force Transitions: Uptight improvisers resist change (especially change that is provoked by their partner). Force transitions by shouting: 'Recognize her!', or: 'Faint!', or: 'Show him a photograph!', or: 'Weep!', or: 'Pounce on her and apologize!', and so on.

Explore Latent Material: Instead of exploring the material they already have, most improvisers prefer to drag in new ideas, i.e. they try to avoid the obvious in favour of something 'original'. Ask yourself: 'What does the audience want to happen?' and then try to make it happen. If a husband and wife have been pretending to watch a horror movie on T.V. and are now refusing to develop the theme of horror, shout: 'Hear a strange noise from the basement.'

Combine Elements: If there are two separate items on the stage, the audience will want them to interact, and they'll want to see the players being changed by the interaction. If there is a performer on the stage and a book on the table, say: 'Read something from the book!' (And then say: 'Be altered by what you read!').

Enforce Recapitulation: Structure is achieved by cannibalising events that were described earlier in the scene. The director should remember what has already happened, and get the players to 'feed it back in'. If someone escapes from an axe-murderer and arrives home, say: "Open a cupboard and discover the axe-murderer!" This will make the audience very happy.

Suggest Corrective Games: For example if the player is using gags as a substitute for interaction, make them continue in gibberish, or in three word sentences. If they are refusing to be controlled by each other, make them use He said/She said.

Canceling: If the improvisers build a fire they're likely to introduce a shower of rain that will douse it. Don't let them cancel their work; let a Sasquatch be attracted by the flames, or have them accidentally start a conflagration, or tell them to cook something. «

*Keith Johnstone,
News 5 1993*

Here are some other improviser bad habits and examples of how to direct around them.

Wimping: The improviser tries to stay safe by not committing to an idea or the scene, they avoiding putting themselves at risk of failing. On a date a player asks 'What would you like to do?' they reply 'I don't know?' Both players are wimping. Stop the players and go back, direct one of the players to say: 'I want to read your palm.' or: 'Let me show you what I have in the basement.' or: 'I brought the pre-nup.' or: 'I need you to make love to me.' anything to start interaction or change the other player.

Hedging: Delays the story from moving forward by circling around the obvious but not getting to it. It often appears in long descriptions of people or places or characters talking about what they could or might do. Directors need to move the actors forward. Often something as simple as 'do it', 'get there', 'begin' or 'you arrive' can help move the action along.
Example: a player enters a tomb and says: 'There is Dracula's coffin. Finally I have found it. I will open it and plunge this knife into your heart and free the world of your kind. The great book says…'
The director should shout: 'Open the coffin!' or 'Do it!'.

Sidetracking: Is preventing forward progress of the story, by taking the story on a different track. Example: 'I went to talk to my boss today.' 'Yes, how is he?' 'Good, his son is getting married.' 'You mean Brayden? Oh how wonderful. Why weren't we invited?'. Going to talk to your boss sets the possibility of your security at work and talking about their son's wedding has completely sidetracked that. Stop the scene and bring them back to the 'I went to talk to my boss today.' say: 'Did you get the raise?' or: 'Did you show him the compromising photos we have of him?'.

Gossip: A bit of gossip at the start of a scene can be useful to help set the platform. Gossip by nature is talking about people not there, which isn't very interesting theatre. Directors need to turn gossip into interaction by prompting one of the players to be changed. For example: 'Do you remember Ethel?' 'The girl we went to school with?' 'Yes. She's moved back to town.' the director might say: 'Scream WHAT! She's back???'.

GORILLA THEATRE™
IN MORE DETAIL

How to Move Scenes Forward by Directing / Side Coaching

>> **A computer** that occasionally said 'do it' (instead of talking about it) could be a useful Impro teacher. <<
Keith Johnstone

Scenes often stall when the action or interaction is blocked. Below are some helpful directions you can give to players as a director or side coach to help players move the action forward.

SAK Theatre - Orlando, USA by Emmi Green

Compiled by Dennis Cahill & Shawn Kinley - Loose Moose Theatre Co.

- Be altered - Emotional reaction (i.e. start to cry)
- Don't speak for 15 seconds
- Be positive (or start again being positive)
- Make eye contact or try to make eye contact but are unable to for more than a second
- Touch partner
- Define the relationship
- Heighten i.e. make it worse
- Restart
- Leave
- Tell a secret or have a secret or confess
- Make emotional sounds
- Give reasons i.e. three reasons you can't accept the marriage proposal
- State belief
- Suddenly see something
- "What inspires you?" "What do you fear?" "What do you hate?"
- Alter your status
- In scenes with 3 or 4 people, add hidden pecking order
- Be opposite (and justify the change)
- Surprise yourself (think of something to say, then change it)
- Take a deep breath
- Don't talk about action, just do it
- Contact makes you giggle, feels good, feels like a light electric current
- Slightly bore the audience, but not yourself
- Be positive, but don't do or say anything really interesting for at least a minute
- Discover something that alters the relationship (i.e. a strand of someone else's hair)
- Stop people from entering a scene just when something is going to happen
- Start with one person on, and have someone enter

Ending Scenes

>> If a scene isn't working the directors should try to inspire the improvisers' imagination so they discover what happens next. You could try to interrupt their intellect, have them change emotion, connect them to each other and the scene, give them permission to leap into the unknown, remind them of what they've forgotten or raise the stakes. If nothing is working then find an ending or just end it, claim responsibility as director and admit your directing defeat by taking a forfeit. <<
Patti Stiles
Impro Melbourne, Melbourne, Australia, Loose Moose Theatre, RFT, Die Nasty alumna

Ending an improvisation scene is a challenge for many reasons.

- If scenes start without a strong platform the improvisers will struggle to discover what the scene is about. This results in endings being less obvious.
- If scenes are muddling along and the improvisers suddenly get a laugh they will not see this as an escape hatch. Instead it is like a 'candy reward' and they will continue searching for the next laugh.
- Instead of cutting their losses when a scene is not going well, improvisers will struggle to 'make it work'. This is an example of not embracing failure with good nature.
- Some people love to be on stage and will stay out there regardless of how much they are torturing the audience. Let the lighting improviser end scenes. They have a unique perspective and see the audience's boredom - if you want to continue you can wave the lights up again.

>> **On a good night** everything works splendidly, but on a bad night the directors in Gorilla Theatre™ - in common with most improvisers - will allow boring scenes to grind on pointlessly. Only the most experienced directors have the self-discipline to bail out and cut their losses. We know this, because we've been inviting them to kill their scenes after thirty seconds without incurring a forfeit, and yet even when they know that there is nothing of the slightest interest on the stage, most of them will opt to continue. I'm working on this problem, but in the meantime the players can help by saying, 'Nothing's happening. What should I do?' or 'Help us! We're dying out here!' or 'Do you think anyone is still interested?'. <<   *Keith Johnstone, Impro For Storytellers pg. 46*

Loose Moose Theatre Company - Calgary, Canada
by Breanna Kennedy

Suggestions on How to End Scenes

- Fulfil the promise(s) made to the audience. (A promise is a hope or expectation in the audience's mind)
- Answer the questions in the audience's mind
- Solve the problem or complete the action
- Reincorporate something from the start of the scene
- Make an exit
- Bring the lights down
- Create a 'cliff hanger' and say… to be continued
- Ask the director for help
- Ask the audience what they would like
- Admit defeat

When none of these seem to work…
- Make a gag

>> *Remember that there are times to step in and times to stay out. Be confident and firm in your directions. Avoid any vagueness and make bold decisions.* << *Chris Wells, In The Moment*
Tokyo, Japan

Rationing the Directing Time

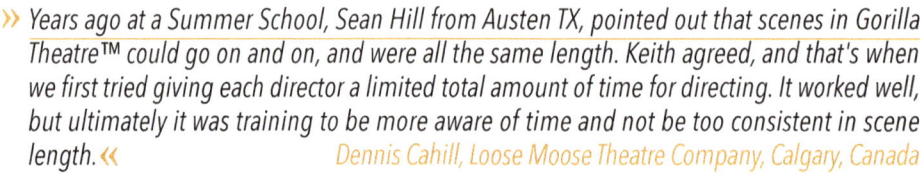

>> *Years ago at a Summer School, Sean Hill from Austen TX, pointed out that scenes in Gorilla Theatre™ could go on and on, and were all the same length. Keith agreed, and that's when we first tried giving each director a limited total amount of time for directing. It worked well, but ultimately it was training to be more aware of time and not be too consistent in scene length.* << *Dennis Cahill, Loose Moose Theatre Company, Calgary, Canada*

You can play a version of the show where each director is given a certain amount of time in the show like chess with a chess clock. Their 'time' begins when they take their turn. So interaction with the audience, scene set up and the scene are included in this time. The emcee should announce how much time a director has left each time the director gets up to take their turn.

>> **Each player** is allowed 20 minutes of directing time (in total), and the Commentator keeps an eye on this, saying, for example, "Ray's scene lasted three minutes and forty seconds - that leaves him 11 minutes of directing time in this game.
This is working well and stops the scenes from dribbling on, but if the players start scheming to win by doing very short scenes I'll have to invent some device to correct this. << *Keith Johnstone*
Impro For Storytellers pg. 47

THE GORILLA

>> *Treat the gorilla at first like a fascinating yet un-predictable creature. Then warm to him (or her) as you all become part of the same team.* << *Steve Jarand*
Loose Moose Theatre, Calgary, Canada

Respect the gorilla. Think of the gorilla as an excellent member of the cast, this is why spending a week with her/him is an honour.

>> **Without a gorilla** the game is just 'My Scene Impro', but a gorilla can add greatly to the 'spectacle'.
"Gorillas spend time backstage cooling off, but they can help with the scenography or they can give hats to the actors or hand them props. They can be in scenes as a 'rug', or an exhibit in the zoo, or a low-key waiter and so on (always in a supporting role). They should fill any dead space between scenes with their antics, perhaps creating pathos when an actor rejects a prop, or applauding when a player they like is rewarded banana after banana.
An obedient gorilla is useless. Gorillas have to misbehave. Encourage them to experiment. Tell them they are expected to take risks and they're allowed at least two big mistakes in each show.
A Gorilla should be a memorable part of the show, but it mustn't become the star. <<   *Keith Johnstone*
Impro For Storytellers pg. 48-49

Playing the Gorilla

The gorilla should be 'gorilla-like' during the show, especially when introduced at the start and when awarding bananas or presenting the forfeit chalice.
When she/he is invited to play in a scene, the gorilla, for example, can walk upright and be an efficient waiter; or they can be a gorilla 'playing' the role of a waiter but still moving in a gorilla-like manner. There is great fun and creative opportunities in both. It could be helpful to use a 'gorilla-ness' scale (1-10) to help gauge how to play. There are times like the show opening and closing when she/he can go wild (8 or 9 on the scale) and other times when the ape element is mostly concealed (2 or 3) like in a scene playing the school principal. Other moments like a walk-through in a park scene or as a gang member she/he might be somewhere between human and animal (4 or 5). This awareness will help the gorilla player pace themself. It can be an exhausting job.
Gorillas are 'knuckle-walkers' so any time they can crouch and be on all fours (even for a moment) they feel more primitive. They can even just 'knuckle' their way across furniture, window frames, etc. When the gorilla does stand up and walk it should feel a bit unstable and awkward. Arms flap around for balance and expression. And don't forget the occasional chest pounding. Cup the hands and try to get a popping sound.
Playful baby behaviour works well like sitting in the middle of the floor, carrying in things on head and shoulders, exploring or tasting things, or knocking stuff over.
Before the show, actors playing the gorilla should put on the suit and look at themselves in a mirror. They should try moving slowly side to side and explore different angles, such as tilting the head and looking down. This helps to understand how the mask's movements and stillness can project emotions and thoughts. Other cast members can sit in the audience and give feedback on which movements/positions project the most feeling, power and truth.

*Unexpected Productions
Seattle, USA*
by Jennifer Matthews

*Loose Moose Theatre Company
Calgary, Canada*
by Breanna Kennedy

GORILLA THEATRE™
IN MORE DETAIL

>> *I love to play Gorilla especially because it is a very good format for variety. You can play different situations and move from an emotion to another quickly. Moreover it has a very funny context, thanks to the gorilla, that naturally helps players to take risks.* << *Giuseppe Marchei*
i Bugardini, Rome, Italy

Performing with the Gorilla

When an improviser reacts to the gorilla like any other player or stage hand, so does the audience. But if every time the ape shows up there is an element of surprise or gratitude, their presence naturally becomes unique and special.

When playing in a scene with the gorilla, players should understand what she/he 'says' or does. Have the gorilla experiment with sound effects: grunts, growls, moans, whimpers and practice giving them meaning. Treat them like they belong in the world of the scene so you can get on with the dramatic action of the scene itself. Resist making comments like: "Nice day today, whoa that guy must be hot." or, "That's one hairy bus driver".

On a practical level, cast members should always be looking out for the gorilla's comfort and safety. It is hot in the costume and difficult to see and hear. Keep an eye on her/him as she/he is entering or leaving the stage especially if the lights are low. Open doors or move curtains when she/he brings things on and off the playing area. If there is someone else playing the role of scenographer, they can double as an informal 'gorilla keeper'.

Impro Melbourne
Melbourne, Australia
📷 *by Impro Melbourne*

Preparing the Costume

>> **Purchase several costumes** and launder them frequently. The 'fur' has to be shaggy. Commercial gorilla costumes can be ordered via carnival shops. <<
Keith Johnstone
Impro For Storytellers pg. 48

The gorilla is an important element of the show, so invest in a good costume. We'd recommend getting a few suits of different sizes. Choose players who fit the fur well. If the actor is a bit tall, make sure they have black clothes underneath in case we see a gap at the neck, wrists or ankles. You might consider removable padding for small or skinny bodies. Sports shoulder pads create a great ape shape.

The head piece is critical. Often they are too big and collapse around the face and neck. It's possible to add foam inside to help keep the shape. Seeing the skin tone of the actor around the eye-holes of the

top:
Impro Melbourne
Melbourne, Australia
📷 by Kevin Yank

gorilla destroys the illusion. Have the actor apply a ring of black make-up around their eyes so the face blends into the mask. You can also add black screen so the eye-holes become shadows. Or add painted eyes that the player looks though or above. Make as many breathing/air holes as possible without revealing any of the player inside.

In scenes the gorilla can wear costume pieces. Have some ready that you know are big enough to fit over the suit.

Detto Fatto
Turin, Italy
📷 by Andrea Pittana

Not Using a Gorilla

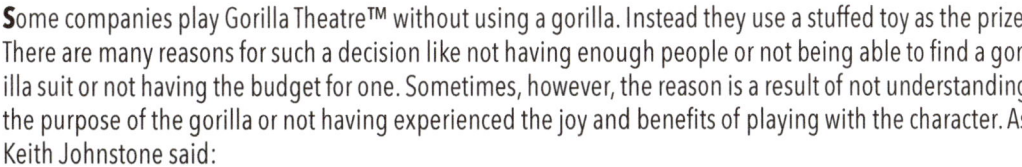

》 *I love the way that the silent gorilla encourages variety, and less 'talky' scenes.* 《
Jarrad Parker, On The Fly, Adelaide, Australia

Some companies play Gorilla Theatre™ without using a gorilla. Instead they use a stuffed toy as the prize. There are many reasons for such a decision like not having enough people or not being able to find a gorilla suit or not having the budget for one. Sometimes, however, the reason is a result of not understanding the purpose of the gorilla or not having experienced the joy and benefits of playing with the character. As Keith Johnstone said:
"Without a gorilla the game reverts to 'My Scene Impro', but a gorilla adds to the 'spectacle'."
The gorilla offers a dynamic theatrical device, for example, explore a scene on bullying or exclusion with the gorilla being 'different' from everyone else. The audience projects what they think the difference implied in the scene is i.e: racist, sexist, or religious bias.
The gorilla exhibits visual variety presenting the bananas or forfeits, or each time she/he makes another appearance. It reminds the audience we are in the theatre, a place of imagination and play.
We encourage groups to explore playing Gorilla Theatre™ with the gorilla.

It is useful to think of the gorilla as a mask character. For more information about this see the Mask section in Attention to Detail on page 45.

GORILLA THEATRE™
IN MORE DETAIL

>> *One night Jenny Lovell set me in a scene with the gorilla. 'One of you has a gambling addiction. You went into a casino 'only for 5 minutes' on a 35 degree (celsius) day leaving your baby in the car. Now you and your spouse are in the emergency waiting room, waiting for news about your child.' Jaime Cerda (the gorilla) understood how to play a mask so the audience could project their own morality and imagination onto this character. The scene had the audience in tears as we tackled the theme of gambling addiction and its impact on people's lives. The next day I was replaying this scene in my mind and I smiled thinking 'We moved the audience to feel, cry and think while they watched a man in a gorilla suit.'* <<

Patti Stiles , Impro Melbourne, Melbourne, Australia
Loose Moose Theatre, RFT, Die Nasty alumna

DRAWING HEAT

>> *I always love when a director isn't happy with how the scene is being played, and it allows for a moment of heat while the improvisers try hard to either please the director or playfully go the other direction.* <<

Dave Ware, Loose Moose Theatre Company
Calgary, Canada

>> **Heat is a wrestling term** meaning uproar among the crowd, and wrestlers create it by self aggrandizement, and by seeming to pummel their perfectly healthy but heavily bandaged arm. << *Keith Johnstone*

>> *When Keith suggested the concept of creating "heat" in Gorilla Theatre™ it opened up a whole new way of playing with the audience. I love being the bad guy and making the audience boo me or sometimes punish me with a forfeit that I might not otherwise have deserved. It adds a whole new dimension to Gorilla Theatre™."* <<

Dennis Cahill, Loose Moose Theatre Company, Calgary, Canada

Picnic Impro - Bogota Colombia   by Fernanda Pineda

» **In Gorilla Theatre™** heat is usually generated by the performers' behaviour between scenes and by their interaction with the 'directors'. Players give the audience permission to boo and cheer by making themselves 'targets', for example by making mocking, confident or arrogant announcements like:
"You thought that was a good scene? Wait until you see this one!" or
"Now I'll show you something with emotional truth and power." or
"I will entrust you to do this scene even though you totally screwed up the previous one!" or
"When this scene is over you will have the privilege of pinning the banana on me!"
The audience will be ready to punish you; and yet, if the scene is good they'll be just as eager to 'banana you'.
If you receive a forfeit you might incite the audience further by saying:
"What for? You were laughing! You were crying! You were being entertained!"
Sometimes one of the players will be a 'baddie' who says aggressive things like:
"That scene was worth a whole bunch of bananas. It wasn't? Who said that? Don't think you won't find your tires slashed when you leave the theatre!"
Asked to make the audience weep, the players stood about looking miserable, yet when the director was greeted by screams of forfeit he pretended to be indignant.
"Well, the scene didn't make us weep." shouted an audience member.
"I'll make you weep!" shouted the director, with fake belligerence. Later on he was booed by some audience members as he was accepting his banana so he said: "You're all together now, but remember this – it'll be dark when you leave the building!" The threat was greeted with ecstatic cheers, and cries of 'take his banana away'.
Observe how professional wrestlers excite their audience by pretending to be bestial, and / or lunatically arrogant.
It has to be clear that the players are just 'teasing' and that their fake 'aggression' is an expression of good-nature. «
Keith Johnstone, Gorilla and Maestro Newsletter '98

Drawing Heat is understanding how to play to get a response from the audience, like wrestlers. This is all to make an audience playfully hate you (playful in the context of the show where we know it is a game) or to have them cheer you on.
Perhaps it is useful to think of it along the lines of a villain in a children's theatre production or a pantomime where the audience is encouraged to yell, boo and hiss you. Everyone knows it is part of the show but loves joining in the roar of 'boo' or the ecstasy of your success.
Directors can have different personalities or relationships with each other and the audience that helps to generate Heat (or audience like / dislike) and adds to variety of the show. Drawing heat this way does not mean the directors should dress as characters. It is demonstrated in their behaviour. The Heat or 'personalities' are not the 'show' they are elements of the show.
Those who play with fear, or actually want to win, will find drawing Heat difficult. Knowing how and when to draw Heat requires skill and practice. It is more challenging than it sounds.

THE EMCEE (MASTER OF CEREMONIES)

>> **When the scene ends** the player least involved - certainly not the director – becomes the emcee. <<
Keith Johnstone

Playing the format with the players emceeing the game as a team requires them to be aware of every aspect of the show at all times including taking votes. Improvisers who are not confident in their performing and directing skills may find this added responsibility too much, so for beginners, a designated emcee may be the best option.

Unexpected Productions - Seattle, USA — by Jennifer Matthews

The emcee players do the following:
- Welcome the audience
- Introduce players
- Explain the show, the voting and what directors are competing for
- Run a sample vote
- Introduce the gorilla
- Conduct the vote between scenes
- Do a banana count at the start of the second half
- Announce the winner at the end of the evening
- Thank the audience

It is important that the emcee, or the players in the role, be charming, warm and efficient and that they do not see the emcee function as part of the entertainment. It is a job that provides the audience with the information they need to follow the show, keeps it flowing and supports the improvisers who are creating the entertainment.

VOTING

>> *The most important elements are 1. The banana or forfeit, because it takes the pressure of failing out of the improvisers. 2. The 'competition' between the directors, it gives the audience a nice feeling of sports, really wanting someone to win or just enjoying the forfeits when failing.* <<
Felipe Ortiz, Picnic Impro, Bogota, Colombia

Gorilla Theatre™ differs from shows like SuperScene or Director's Cut in that the audience is voting on the success or failure of the director not the quality of the scene or story.
Improvisers are off the hook (or feel less pressure) because the vote is not for them.
The spectators need to be rehearsed in shouting BANANA and FORFEIT at the beginning of the show (or courteous spectators may be reluctant to yell 'forfeit').
You might say: "If you thought the director directed their scene well you'd yell 'banana', if you felt the director did not direct the scene well you'd yell 'forfeit'. Let's practice. Imagine Steve directed a scene well. On

the count of three yell 'banana', one... two... three (pause for audience to yell 'banana'). Now let's say Patti failed in her directing duties, you'd yell 'forfeit', lets try it, one... two... three (pause for audience to yell 'forfeit')."
You could split the audience in two: "Let's say this side didn't like how Sarah directed, they will yell 'forfeit'. This side did and they will yell 'banana'. One... two... three. (audience yells)."
There are different ways of holding the vote. Your aim is to have it structured so the players can make a decision, but not so structured that the audience feels they are in school and have to be obedient. You want a nice 'roar' of voices that encourages a release of energy in contrast to 'raise your hands' which stifles the release.

Impro Melbourne, Melbourne, Australia
by John Desengano

A few voting styles:
1. You separate the vote. Do a vote for banana and then a vote for forfeit.
2. Have the audience yell either 'banana or 'forfeit' at the same time.
Here is Keith's suggestion...

>> **Did so-and-so** direct that scene badly? On the count of three - One! Two! Three!' He or she then asks, "Did so and so direct that scene well?" (Always do negative first, positive second, and never say 'was that scene worth a banana' or the audience will vote for the scene, and not for the directing of it.) If the roar is undecipherable, take the vote again. When in doubt say 'It sounds like banana has the edge over forfeit.' <<
Keith Johnstone

BANANAS

>> *As a director, the focus is on supporting the players' Impro, rather than getting a banana.* <<
Jarrad Parker, On The Fly, Adelaide, Australia

A banana is the reward for successfully directing your scene.

>> **The pinning** of the first banana should be an important moment. Subsequent bananas can be more casual, but the pinning should always happen on stage – the spectators like to see their Hero honoured. Never pin a banana onto yourself; another player (or the gorilla) must do it for you. Don't 'bunch' the bananas or it'll be difficult to 'read' which director is ahead. <<
Keith Johnstone, Impro For Storytellers pg. 43

If wearing the bananas is not an option you could create a scoreboard. The scoreboard should clearly and cleanly state the players names, display the bananas they have won and be easily readable from the audience. After intermission have a 'banana count' to remind the audience of the stakes in the game.

Contemporary Theater Company
Rhode Island, USA by Neal Leaheey

FORFEITS

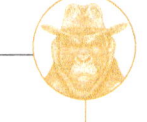

» *For me one of the most interesting elements of Gorilla is the forfeit. It is a possibility to be silly or truthful in a one to one relationship with the audience. It's also an excellent tool for other improvisers to work on supporting you when support is needed.* «
Daniel Orrnatia
Picnic Impro, Bogota, Colombia

A forfeit is the punishment for not successfully directing your scene.

» **These should be much shorter** than the scenes and they should provide a contrast with the scenes – they should not include Impro games. The forfeits are written on pieces of paper and put into the 'forfeit chalice' before the game. Any forfeit a player objects to is removed beforehand. If, when the moment comes, you decide you don't want to do a particular forfeit, read out something else, i.e. 'cheat'. «
Keith Johnstone
Gorilla and Maestro Newsletter '98

» *If you mess up the scene - the forfeits are a built-in mechanism to cleanse the palate and for the audience to feel as though justice has been served.* «
Cam Percy, Impro Mafia
Brisbane, Australia

DettoFatto-italy
Turin, Italy
by Andrea Pittana

Tokyo Comedy Store
Tokyo, Japan
by Allan McIntyre

Creating Forfeits

» *Forfeits have to be more than opportunities to show off, they have to have some small element of humiliation. Forfeits where there is a success or failure are tricky (recite the alphabet backwards) because what happens if you fail? Do you get another forfeit? (No.) Forfeits which involve personal revelation are good. "Tell us the thing you've done of which you are most ashamed." You don't have to tell the truth necessarily.* «
Tom Salinsky, Spontaneity Shop
London, UK

Forfeits should:
· Be in the spirit of good nature
· Be accepted fearlessly by the improviser
· Be seen by the audience as a 'punishment'
· Be a moment that adds contrast to the show
· Be an example of something you'd never see in traditional theatre
· Mostly happen in the moment or during the evening

Forfeits should not:
· Be a long scene
· Be an Impro game
· Be stupid, embarrassing, hurtful or belittling to the performer

》 **If the forfeit** asks you to apologize for your existence, please be sincere. 《
Keith Johnstone
Gorilla and Maestro Newsletter '98

Forfeit Tips

》 *Embrace failure. Commit to absolutely everything - especially your forfeits. The show can't be all bananas, or there's no shape to it.* 《   *Jarrad Parker, On The Fly, Adelaide, Australia*

· Have a wide array of 'types' of forfeits for variety in the show.
· Invent new forfeits from time to time including ones that relate to current or local events.
· Alternate your forfeits and be mindful you are not using the same forfeits each week. Maybe make a list of the ones you've done and pull them from the forfeit chalice the following week.
· Watch the urge to start creating stupid or embarrassing forfeits.

A List of Useful Forfeits

· Stride arrogantly about the stage as the audience 'Boo and Hiss'
· Redirect that miserable scene till it works
· Apologize to every member of the audience as they leave the theatre at the end of the show
· Do ten pushups (players can adjust to physical abilities and for fun you could ask the audience to count like a drill Sergeant)
· Give a eulogy for your deceased scene
· Phone your parents (or a close friend) and tell them about the wretched scene you just directed
· Improvise an epic poem until the audience begs you to stop
· Ask God to make you a better director

GORILLA THEATRE™
IN MORE DETAIL

i Bugardini - Rome, Italy 📷 *by Elisa Pizza*

· Expose a personal secret
· Become very old and reminisce about your days as a young improviser
· Take a picture of yourself with a disapproving audience member
· Lose a banana to a player chosen by the audience
· Run around the theatre yelling "I can do better!!!"
· Walk an audience member to their car after the show
· Have an audience member leave you a voicemail reminding you how badly you directed
· Break up with yourself
· Work bar at intermission
· Apologize sincerely to the audience
· Have audience members beat you with balloons (or foam stick pool noodles)
· Give an inspirational speech to the players to rally their faith in you after your failure
· Run to the store across the street and bring the front row a treat like doughnuts (this inspires people to sit in the front row... Have the treat ready back stage)

WINNING

Impro Melbourne
Melbourne, Australia
📷 *by Impro Melbourne*

》 **Improvisation** should be an expression of good nature. 《   *Keith Johnstone*

》 Winning the gorilla ought to be approached as the opportunity to spend a week with your favourite person. It's not something to be indifferent about, but it's also not something to act like a madman about either - that would be creepy and off-putting. Endow the gorilla with value - something that you'd really, really enjoy. 《   *Rebecca Northan, Spontaneous Theatre, Toronto, Canada*
Loose Moose Theatre alumna

At the end of the show the player with the most bananas wins. This should be a celebration and should honour the achievement of the director in the eyes of the audience. Please do not put any silly costume pieces on them, it embarrasses the player and trivializes the triumph. The other directors should shake the winners hand in the spirit of goodwill. The gorilla reappears and the show closes as the director and gorilla leave hand in hand, or one carrying the other, to begin the aforementioned 'week of quality time'.

》 We give to the gorilla honour and relevance. We try to give the audience the feeling that it is really important for directors to win the night in order to have the opportunity to have its special time with gorilla. 《   *Giuseppe Marchei, i Bugardini, Rome Italy*

Loose Moose Theatre Company - Calgary, Canada by Breanna Kennedy

ATTENTION TO DETAIL

Tips on Training Gorilla Directors
by Tom Salinsky

Teaching people to play Gorilla Theatre™; in my experience people tend to go through the following stages when directing.
INACTION. People barely contribute at all beyond setting up the scene.
OVER-DIRECTING. The improvisers are denied almost all autonomy as the new director over-corrects the previous error.
APPROPRIATE DIRECTING. Directors learn how and when to intervene to make the scene better, and when to leave it alone. But they don't fight for their vision. I sometimes call this "Maestro Directing" because in Maestro, the directors are (should be) trying to get the best out of the players. It's usually better if they don't have a vision for the scene, because it's not their show. But directors at this stage are playing "Round Robin Maestro". They aren't fighting for the vision, and so there are no "crash-and-burns".
ALL FIGHTING ALL THE TIME. After a couple of experiences, players get a taste for the sheer joy of the crash and burn chaos and pretty soon, almost every scene goes this way.
APPROPRIATE GORILLA THEATRE™ DIRECTING. Finally, they settle down and start aiming for a reasonable ratio of strong scenes to chaos (about 3:1 I think is good) and also are happy to wait for an opportunity rather than forcing a scene to go off the rails, either as player or as director.
This process can take up to a year.

Tips on Directing
by Shawn Kinley - excerpts from several ITI Newsletters

Move the performers towards relationship. Amazingly, we avoid deepening connections on stage all the time. If the performers are a master and servant in a castle, take a step further and bring the relationship closer. "Tell your servant you've been watching him sleeping at night." "Tell your master you have fallen in love with her." "Tell your servant that you are actually his father".
And even with what might seem non-human relationships - bring the relationship closer. The pigeon has a message around its leg that you read. The old picture on the wall is not random, it looks like you, your mother, your best friend. One night when you pray, a voice answers you.
MOVE FORWARD - Many improvisers are delaying the action because they are scared. (scared to define, scared to show emotion, scared to improvise). If a gun is pulled, it had better be fired or cause a strong reaction. If you've been standing at the foot of a mountain or entrance to a cave you had better climb or go in. Listen to the audience whispers. You sometimes hear the voices. You occasionally hear audience members say "DO IT!" where promises have been made and delayed. Move forward where promises are implied or directly spoken.
DEFINE... Watch performances and listen for words like 'things', 'stuff', 'I don't know'. When the performer

is scared to define, the scene can't move forward. Give the pet a name. Sebastian the bull mastiff is much better than feeding 'the pet'. Climbing Mount Sinister implies a lot more than just climbing that generic mountain.

ACTIONS - Move performers towards actions rather than words. eg: having an improviser climb out on the window ledge is more interesting than an improviser telling his boss that he is depressed and angry about being fired.

Impro Melbourne
Melbourne, Australia
by Impro Melbourne

ADD THEATRICALITY AND SPECTACLE TO THE SHOW

It is exciting to give your Gorilla Theatre™ teammates or the director inspiring material to work with. Here are a few suggestions to boost the expressiveness and theatricality of the show.

Masks

Playing Masks
As we mentioned earlier, the gorilla is essentially a mask character. As well as half and full masks, masks used for scenes could come in the form of costume pieces like wigs, hats and glasses or partial masks like beards, moustaches, eyebrows, teeth, noses or cheeks. The idea is to take inspiration from the feeling of transformation. You are free of responsibility because the "Mask" takes over.

It can take some practice to play in a scene with a mask but there are a few keys into a good experience. One thing is to accept that the mask (or special person) is likely the focus. Other improvisers can take comfort in the role of facilitating and enlivening their journey. This doesn't mean that you passively accept and follow whatever the mask wants. It could be that they need some challenge, resistance, mystery and play like any other improviser. Acting with a mask can be a bit like acting out a play with a four year old. You care that they look good and have a great time but could likely not improve on their imagination.

Loose Moose Theatre Company - Calgary, Canada by Kate Ware

Directing Masks
Similar guidelines apply for directing as when playing along side masks. In addition a director needs to be extra clear and confident both for the character to understand the elements of the scene and so that the player is free to remain immersed in the experience of partial trance that the mask allows.

Full masks are wonderful tools to help in the training of directors. Out of necessity, the world of the full mask must be as clear and simple as possible otherwise (without words) the relationship and story become confused or needlessly abstract. Therefore directors can set up simple situations with clear problems or dilemmas in order to spark an emotional voyage for the character and audience as well. (Goodbyes, fresh love, moral dilemmas, questioning faith/sanity).

Sensory skills can easily be cultivated if a director allows her or himself to see what is obvious. Not only does it seem to the audience that a director is incredibly perceptive when they make use of what is already evident onstage, but it also informs the mask player about who they are and what the impression is on the other side of the face. If there is one prop on stage like a stuffed animal for example, plus a table and a door, then sitting on the chair holding the stuffy and looking at the door is a great start, or perhaps a great ending.

For more information on training and playing masks read the Mask and Trance chapter in Keith Johnstone's book Impro and be sure to look at our resources section at the end of the guide.

*Loose Moose Theatre Company
Calgary, Canada
by Kate Ware*

SCENOGRAPHY

Scenography is the art of supporting players and their scenes by enhancing the environment with props, furniture, cloth material and other objects. Scenographers are sometimes lovingly called 'Snoggers' ('snogging' is also slang for kissing).

Gorilla theatre™ is a good place to cultivate these skills and the ensemble can take turns 'snogging' for each other or one or two other improvisers can have that exclusive role for the evening.

Here are some examples of scenographic support:
· Create a living room or office when the scene calls for it (three chairs covered with a blanket as a sofa, a box for a table if no table is available etc.)
· Add the extra characters that can embellish a restaurant, archaeological dig etc.
· Make people fly by simply lifting them
· Alter the physical perspective of the scene to enhance the narrative by creating a tiny village with fingers for monsters to trample

*Impro Melbourne
Melbourne, Australia
by Fiona Anderson*

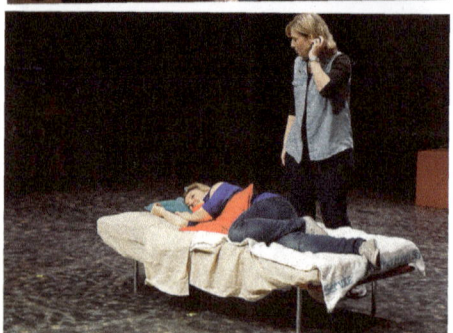

*Impro Melbourne
Melbourne, Australia
by John Desengano*

At the Loose Moose Theatre, scenography developed greater relevance with improvisers Tom Lamb and Shawn Kinley who took the technical aspect of moving furniture for efficiency and transformed it into creating vivid images with simple objects found backstage. Shawn mentioned, "We felt good when we saw the improvisers light up with inspiration because of something we offered."

Scenography is a strong teacher of improvisation. The scenographer is always looking for ways to support the scene and the players or to enhance the show. These are useful skills for any improviser.

For example you could 'use your bodies' to become the necessary objects and characters or 'practice adapting' by exploring your available environment and turning it into other realities. What can you do with a chair? - a walker, a jack-hammer, a beach chair (on it's back), a giant's feet (that other players help you to walk with?)

Loose Moose Theatre Company
Calgary, Canada
by Kate Ware

Useful set pieces for Snoggers, if budget and space allow:
· A couch (with a hole that you can dive into and disappear)
· A bed (that you can dive into and disappear)
· Table & chairs
· Wheelchair
· Picnic blanket
· Plastic trees
· Tombstone (made of styrofoam)
· Boat

Not every theatre group or company has access to a wide array of props so workshops have been developed around adapting scenography to the available tools at hand.

Here are some ideas:

"Scenography in a suitcase". A simple case or box full of collapsible and adaptable objects can make it look like you have 10 times more props than you actually have. (Solid coloured material becomes a cape, screen, river, etc., white cloth over a chair makes a throne in heaven, umbrellas become trees, radar dishes, etc…). You don't need much storage space for a suitcase of well-chosen props.

Impro Melbourne
Melbourne, Australia
by Impro Melbourne

Loose Moose Theatre Company
Calgary, Canada
by Breanna Kennedy

Loose Moose Theatre Company - Calgary, Canada by Breanna Kennedy

FINAL THOUGHTS

Gorilla Theatre™ is an exciting format that will challenge and develop your skills while allowing you to create dynamic improvisational theatre. It isn't an easy format but can be a very rewarding one. Working with people and companies who play and understand the format can be very helpful. Enjoy!

TIPS FROM GROUPS PLAYING GORILLA

"Practice all the extremes:
· Directing players who make lots of strong offers
· Experiments with misbehaviour
· Forfeits out of your comfort zone
· Abandoning or re-forming your scene vision"
Steve Jarand, Loose Moose Theatre Company, Calgary, Canada

"The format structure allows for a lot of fun. The gorilla, the mischief, forfeits, running to the board to put your name up and so forth. Be careful these elements don't become the energy of the show. The structure is there to support risk and exploration by making failure fun. If you are not focused on the scene work and only focused on making the structure as 'funny' as possible, then the show is like a sugary energy drink and pointless."
Patti Stiles, Impro Melbourne, Melbourne, Australia, Loose Moose Theatre, RFT, Die Nasty alumna

"Use the gorilla on stage for a couple of scenes, in order to create expectation. Keep the moments for the directors with a light atmosphere. Have fun!"
Simone Bonetti, Zoè Teatri, Modena, Italy

"It often has a slower pace, which I like. As I've gotten older, I prefer the opportunity to tell better stories, in longer scenes. Gorilla almost lends itself to medium-form improv. At the same time, the faux-competition between directors, and taking the responsibility for the scenes off the performers is pleasurable. I like seeing directors fight for their 'vision', even when it's failing."
Rebecca Northan, Spontaneous Theatre, Toronto, Canada, Loose Moose Theatre alumna

"Directing is a skill - so rehearse it a lot during your regular workshops or rehearsals!"
Chris Wells, Tokyo, Japan

"Learning to direct well is at least as difficult as learning to improvise on stage, so it's going to take time. If I were to give one tip, I'd say that most directors should do more, rather than less. Many directors are usually a bit hesitant to interrupt, and it is easy to become stressed and at a loss of ideas, in the same way improvisers do. If you learn to trust your instincts enough to interrupt the scene, even if you don't know what you are going to say or do, you will start to improve."
Emil Husby, Improoperatørene, Trondheim, Norway

"Keep your scenes shorter than you think they should be. Direct a variety of games/scenes instead of just a few you're confident about, and don't get so locked in to what YOU want to do that you ignore what the SHOW needs next."
Dave Ware, Loose Moose Theatre Company, Calgary, Canada

"We've been playing this format for a while now and I think directors tend to excel when they embrace their own unique quirks and style. No two directors are probably going to direct a scene in the same fashion, or are attracted to the same type of themes and scenic devices. This ability to embrace a wide variety of styles and approaches is one of the biggest gifts of Gorilla."
David Charles, SAK Theatre, Orlando, USA

MEMORABLE GORILLA MOMENTS

"I had the unique experience of playing a half "trance" mask for a whole Gorilla show. He was player as well as director just like the other improvisers.
Here's what I can remember and what others said about having "Francois" in charge of scenes:
· He looks for the conflict to be as strong and as obvious as possible.
· He watches enraptured when it is going well and reacts audibly.
· He loves to jump up and change things or yell when the wrong choices are made.
· It's like a 5 year old whose world is complete and knows exactly how it should go."
Steve Jarand, Loose Moose Theatre Company, Calgary, Canada

"There was a scene with a woman in Berlin who was hiding her violin under her seat. We saw it and asked if she would be the neighbour practicing her instrument. It was a memorable love scene."
Shawn Kinley, Loose Moose Theatre Company, Calgary, Canada

FINAL THOUGHTS

"I do remember a show where one player was misbehaving so much that the others decided together to throw him out of the show. The good part of the story is that this player was so benevolent and charming that he still managed to win, even though he wasn't allowed to direct any scenes for a good part of the show!"
Emil Husby, Improoperatørene, Trondheim, Norway

"One of our directors called his mother on speaker phone to apologize for the bad scene he directed. She had just the right spirit - "shame on you!" - and the audience was beside themselves."
Cam Percy, Impro Mafia, Brisbane, Australia

"At an international tournament in the Netherlands, Deborah was attempting to get the other boys on the stage to play my father truthfully, but they kept making jokes, so she kept firing them. Eventually, she replaced them with an old man from the audience who spoke very little English. Since I had no Dutch, I had to play it as an English/Gibberish scene, but the mainly bilingual audience understood both sides, and loved it when I guessed correctly what was being said and loved it even more when I got it totally wrong."
Tom Salinsky, Spontaneity Shop, London, UK

"Inviting an older audience member on stage to receive an apology for the scene and having her deny forgiveness."
Steve Jarand, Loose Moose Theatre Company, Calgary, Canada

"I think we often bring ourselves and elements of our lives to the stage, such as parenting, dating, work stresses and the like, which can result in both comedic but also revealing and poignant scenic work. A company member, Mike Carr, directed a soundtrack scene to Five for Fighting's "100 Years" that spanned the life of a character in pantomime resulting in him uttering his final breath. It was a really joy-inspired series of called flashbacks that also had a bittersweet taste as the scene closed."
David Charles, SAK Theatre, Orlando, USA

MITICO Festival and ITI conference
Milan, Italy
by Tiffany Schultz

RESOURCES

Keith Johnstone's Books	· IMPRO Improvisation and the Theatre
	· IMPRO For STORYTELLERS
	  Chapter 3 pages 42 - 48
	  http://www.keithjohnstone.com/writing/
	  http://theatresports.com/keiths-books/

Keith Johnstone's Newsletters	· 'Gorilla and Micetro' November 1998 · News 5 1993 → Newsletters are available through the ITI
DVDs	· Impro Transformations · Trance Masks http://www.keithjohnstone.com/video/

Workshops & Training	· Keith Johnstone Impro intensives
	  www.keithjohnstone.com
	· Loose Moose Theatre International Summer School
	  www.loosemoose.com
	· ITI teacher list
	  http://theatresports.com/teachers/

Biographical information	· Keith Johnstone - A Critical Biography by Theresa Robbins Dudeck
	· The Keith Johnstone Papers
	  http://library.stanford.edu/blogs/special-collections-un-bound/2014/07/archives-acquires-keith-johnstone-papers#sthash.cv08mPC7.dpuf
	· Questions about the "Keith Johnstone Papers" or inquiries about Johnstone's literary works, contact Theresa Robbins Dudeck, Literary Executor for Keith Johnstone.
	· Theresa Robbins Dudeck trdudeck@gmail.com
	  http://theresarobbinsdudeck.com/

Gorilla Mask

Impro Melbourne is fortunate to have a player who created a handmade mask specifically for Gorilla Theatre™. The mask is capable of portraying a neutral state and yet is expressive and a strong character when animated by the performer (see phote below). If you are interested in having a mask made for your show, here is some more information:
Description: Handmade Gorilla Performance Mask
Materials: Fibreglass, faux fur, fabric and paint (The fibreglass is ideal for durability, ease of cleaning, and hygiene.)
Contact:
Patrick Duffy (Melbourne, Australia) patrick@cleverfool.com
Price upon application

 We hope you'll enjoy playing Gorilla Theatre™.

Impro Melbourne - Melbourne, Australia by Impro Melbourne

If you have any questions please contact the ITI Email: office@theatresports.org

www.ingramcontent.com/pod-product-compliance
Lightning Source LLC
Chambersburg PA
CBHW061936290426
44113CB00025B/2931